Lights, Camera, Action: A Student's Handbook to Film Production and Directing

Helena Koskinen

Copyright © [2023]

Title: Lights, Camera, Action: A Student's Handbook to Film Production and Directing

Author's: Helena Koskinen.

This book was printed and published by [Publisher's: Helena Koskinen] in [2023]

ISBN:

TABLE OF CONTENTS

Chapter 1: Introduction to Film Production and Directing   06

The Importance of Film Production and Directing

The Role of a Film Director

The Benefits of Studying Film Production and Directing

Chapter 2: Pre-production   13

Understanding the Script

Creating a Storyboard

Developing a Shot List

Casting and Auditions

Securing Locations and Permits

Chapter 3: Production   23

Setting up the Film Set

Camera Techniques and Movements

Lighting Techniques

Directing Actors

Sound Recording

Chapter 4: Post-production 33

Importing and Organizing Footage

Editing Software and Techniques

Adding Visual Effects and Graphics

Sound Editing and Mixing

Color Grading and Finalizing the Film

Chapter 5: Distribution and Promotion 43

Film Festivals and Competitions

Creating a Film Marketing Plan

Utilizing Social Media and Online Platforms

Film Distribution Options

Building a Portfolio and Resume

Chapter 6: Case Studies 54

Analyzing Successful Film Productions

Examining the Directing Styles of Renowned Directors

Learning from Film Production Mistakes

Collaborating with a Film Crew

Showcasing Student Film Projects

Chapter 7: Resources and Further Learning 64

Recommended Books and Websites

Film Production and Directing Courses

Joining Film Clubs and Organizations

Networking Opportunities

Internships and Job Opportunities in the Film Industry

Chapter 8: Conclusion 74

Reflecting on the Journey of Film Production and Directing

Continuing to Grow as a Filmmaker

Inspiring Others through Film

Final Thoughts and Words of Encouragement

Chapter 1: Introduction to Film Production and Directing

The Importance of Film Production and Directing

Lights, Camera, Action: A Student's Handbook to Film Production and Directing

Introduction:

Welcome to the exciting world of film production and directing! In this subchapter, we will explore the importance of these two essential components of filmmaking. Whether you are a film and media studies student or simply someone passionate about the art of cinema, understanding the significance of film production and directing is crucial for your journey in this industry.

The Collaborative Process:

Film production and directing are inherently collaborative processes that bring together a diverse group of individuals to transform a screenplay into a visual and auditory masterpiece. As a student, it is crucial to comprehend the intricacies of this process, as it will allow you to effectively communicate and collaborate with your team members in the future.

Creative Control:

Film production and directing grant you creative control over every aspect of the film. From selecting the right actors, designing sets, crafting the perfect shot, to guiding the overall narrative, you have the power to shape the story and evoke emotions in your audience. Understanding the importance of this creative control empowers you to make informed decisions that align with your artistic vision.

Visual Storytelling:

Film is a powerful medium that allows us to tell stories visually. As a director, you will learn to use various techniques such as camera angles, lighting, sound design, and editing to convey emotions, themes, and messages to your audience. By mastering the art of visual storytelling, you can transport viewers into new worlds, provoke thought, and leave a lasting impact on their lives.

Career Opportunities:

Film production and directing offer a plethora of exciting career opportunities. From independent filmmaking to working in the Hollywood film industry, your skills will be in demand across various platforms such as movies, television shows, documentaries, and commercials. By understanding the importance of film production and directing, you can pave the way for a successful career in the field of your passion.

Conclusion:

In conclusion, film production and directing are integral components of the filmmaking process. As a student in film and media studies, it is vital to recognize the significance of these disciplines to excel in your chosen career path. Whether you aspire to be a director, producer, cinematographer, or editor, understanding the importance of film production and directing will guide you towards achieving your goals.

So, grab your camera, assemble your team, and embark on the journey of creating compelling stories that will captivate audiences worldwide.

The Role of a Film Director

In the captivating world of filmmaking, the director is often regarded as the captain of the ship. They hold the vision, the creative genius, and the ability to bring a script to life on the big screen. As students of film and media studies, it is essential to understand the crucial role a film director plays in the production process.

First and foremost, the film director is responsible for interpreting the screenplay and translating it into a visual narrative. They work closely with the screenwriter to develop a deep understanding of the story, characters, and themes. This collaboration allows the director to envision the overall tone, style, and mood of the film.

Once the vision is established, the director becomes the driving force behind every aspect of the production. They work alongside the production team, including the cinematographer, production designer, and costume designer, to ensure that the visual elements align with their artistic vision. The director also collaborates with the actors, guiding them to deliver performances that bring the characters to life and convey the desired emotions on screen.

During filming, the director must possess exceptional organizational skills. They create shot lists, storyboards, and shot plans to effectively communicate their vision to the crew. They oversee the technical aspects of the production, including camera angles, lighting, and sound, to ensure that each shot captures the intended emotion and enhances the storytelling.

Furthermore, the director is responsible for maintaining the overall pace and rhythm of the film. They make critical decisions about the editing process, working closely with the film editor to shape the story and create a seamless flow. The director's role continues even after the shooting is complete, as they work closely with the post-production team to oversee the final touches, such as color grading and sound design.

In addition to their technical skills, film directors must possess strong leadership qualities. They must effectively communicate their vision to the entire team, inspire creativity, and provide guidance and feedback throughout the production process. They are the ultimate decision-makers, responsible for shaping the film's final product.

As students of film and media studies, understanding the multifaceted role of a film director is vital for pursuing a career in the industry. By studying the works of renowned directors and analyzing their techniques, students can gain an appreciation for the artistry and creative vision required to excel in this profession.

Ultimately, the film director is the driving force behind a film's success. Their ability to bring a script to life, collaborate with a talented team, and make critical decisions at every stage of production is what separates a good film from a great one. So, embrace the role of the director, explore your creativity, and let your vision shine through the lens of the camera.

The Benefits of Studying Film Production and Directing

Lights, Camera, Action: A Student's Handbook to Film Production and Directing

Lights, Camera, Action: A Student's Handbook to Film Production and Directing is a comprehensive guide for students interested in pursuing a career in film and media studies. This subchapter, titled "The Benefits of Studying Film Production and Directing," aims to highlight the advantages that come with choosing this field of study.

One of the primary benefits of studying film production and directing is the opportunity to unleash your creativity. Through this course, students are introduced to the art of storytelling, allowing them to explore different narratives and express their ideas visually. They learn how to write scripts, create storyboards, and develop their own unique directing style. This creative freedom fosters a sense of self-expression and allows students to bring their visions to life on the big screen.

Another advantage of studying film production and directing is the chance to work collaboratively. In the film industry, teamwork is crucial, and this course provides students with ample opportunities to collaborate with peers. They learn the importance of effective communication, problem-solving, and leadership skills. Working in a team not only enhances their interpersonal skills but also prepares them for the real-world challenges they may face in the industry.

Additionally, studying film production and directing equips students with technical skills that are highly sought after in the job market. They gain hands-on experience with industry-standard equipment, such as cameras, lighting, and editing software. This practical training helps students develop a strong foundation in the technical aspects of filmmaking, making them competent and confident in their abilities.

Moreover, studying film production and directing exposes students to a wide range of film genres, styles, and techniques. They learn about the history of cinema, exploring the works of renowned directors and understanding the evolution of filmmaking. This knowledge not only enhances their appreciation for the art form but also expands their horizons, allowing them to develop a diverse and well-rounded perspective.

Lastly, studying film production and directing opens doors to various career opportunities. Whether students aspire to become directors, cinematographers, editors, or screenwriters, this course provides them with the necessary skills and knowledge to pursue their dreams. Furthermore, the film industry offers a plethora of job opportunities, both in traditional filmmaking and emerging digital platforms, ensuring a promising and fulfilling career path for students.

In conclusion, the benefits of studying film production and directing are numerous. From fostering creativity and teamwork to developing technical skills and expanding knowledge, this field of study offers students a unique and rewarding experience. So, if you are passionate about film and media studies, grab a camera, and embark on an exciting journey of storytelling and visual artistry.

Chapter 2: Pre-production

Understanding the Script

In the world of film production and directing, the script is the backbone of every successful project. It serves as the blueprint, the roadmap that guides the entire filmmaking process. Whether you're a budding filmmaker or a student of film and media studies, it is crucial to have a solid understanding of the script and its significance in bringing a story to life on the silver screen.

First and foremost, a script is a written document that tells a story through dialogue, actions, settings, and descriptions. It is the written version of the film, capturing the essence of each scene and character. As a student, it is important to study scripts from various genres and time periods to gain a comprehensive understanding of storytelling techniques and conventions.

To fully comprehend a script, one must learn how to analyze its structure. Most scripts are divided into three acts – the setup, confrontation, and resolution. These acts follow a specific narrative arc that creates tension and engages the audience. By dissecting the script and identifying its key plot points, you can gain insights into the story's pacing and structure.

Additionally, understanding character development is crucial when interpreting a script. Characters are the heart and soul of any film, and their journey is what captivates the audience. By analyzing the characters' goals, motivations, and conflicts, you can better understand their actions and how they contribute to the overall story.

Furthermore, a script provides crucial information about the visual elements of a film. It outlines the locations, props, and costumes required for each scene. As a student delving into the world of film and media studies, learning how to interpret these visual cues is essential in understanding the director's vision and the overall aesthetic of the film.

Lastly, studying the script allows you to explore the techniques used by the writer to create engaging dialogue and memorable scenes. By analyzing the script's dialogue, pacing, and subtext, you can gain insights into the writer's style and intentions.

In conclusion, understanding the script is paramount for any student aspiring to be a filmmaker or studying film and media studies. It serves as the foundation upon which a film is built, providing valuable insights into storytelling, character development, visual elements, and dialogue. So grab a script, immerse yourself in its world, and embark on a journey to uncover the secrets of successful filmmaking.

Creating a Storyboard

A storyboard is a visual representation of a film or video project. It serves as a blueprint for the director, cinematographer, and other members of the production team to follow during the shooting process. In this subchapter, we will explore the importance of storyboarding and provide step-by-step instructions on how to create an effective storyboard for your film.

Why is storyboarding important? Well, imagine trying to build a house without a blueprint. You would have no idea how to proceed, and the end result would likely be chaotic and disorganized. Similarly, a film without a storyboard can be confusing and lack coherence. Storyboarding helps you plan each shot, visualize the sequence of events, and ensure that the story flows smoothly from one scene to another.

So, how do you create a storyboard? Let's break it down:

1. Start with a script: Before you can create a storyboard, you need a script. Read through your script carefully, identifying key scenes and moments that need to be visually represented.

2. Divide your script into scenes: Break down your script into individual scenes, assigning each one a number or title. This will help you organize your storyboard and keep track of the sequence.

3. Sketch your shots: For each scene, sketch out the shots you envision. Include details such as camera angles, movements, and any important visual elements. You don't need to be a professional artist; simple stick figures and basic shapes will suffice.

4. Add descriptions and notes: Alongside each shot, write a brief description or note detailing what is happening in the scene. This can include dialogue, character actions, or any other relevant information.

5. Consider shot transitions: Think about how each shot will transition into the next. Is there a specific visual or narrative link between scenes? Make note of these transitions to ensure a seamless flow in your final film.

Remember, your storyboard is a fluid document that can be modified and adjusted as needed. It is a visual tool to help you plan and communicate your creative vision to your team. By creating a detailed and well-thought-out storyboard, you will save time and resources during production and ensure a more cohesive and visually engaging final product.

In conclusion, storyboarding is an essential step in the filmmaking process. It allows you to plan and visualize your film before you even pick up a camera. By following these steps and dedicating time to create a comprehensive storyboard, you will set yourself up for success and create a film that captivates your audience. So, grab a pen and paper, and start storyboarding your next film project!

Developing a Shot List

Lights, Camera, Action: A Student's Handbook to Film Production and Directing

Welcome to the exciting world of film production and directing! In this subchapter, we will explore the crucial step of developing a shot list. As aspiring filmmakers, understanding the importance of shot lists will greatly enhance your ability to effectively plan and execute your vision on set.

A shot list is a detailed breakdown of all the shots you plan to capture during a particular scene or sequence. It serves as a roadmap for your cinematographer, crew, and actors, ensuring everyone is on the same page and working towards a common goal. A well-crafted shot list not only saves time and resources but also allows for creative freedom and experimentation.

To begin developing your shot list, you must first analyze the script or storyboard. Break down each scene into its individual shots, considering the desired angles, camera movement, and composition. Consider the emotional impact you want to achieve and the story you want to tell through the visuals.

Next, think about the technical aspects of each shot, such as the lens type, camera height, and lighting requirements. This will help you determine the equipment needed and allow you to collaborate more effectively with your cinematographer and crew.

Remember to consider the pacing and rhythm of your film. By varying shot types and lengths, you can create a dynamic visual experience that keeps the audience engaged. Experiment with different shot sizes, from wide establishing shots to intimate close-ups, to convey different emotions and perspectives.

Communication is key when developing a shot list. Collaborate with your cinematographer and storyboard artist to ensure everyone understands the vision and goals of each shot. Share references, sketches, and visual examples to clarify your expectations.

Finally, be open to adjustments and improvisation on set. Although a shot list provides structure, embracing spontaneity and creative problem-solving can lead to unexpected and exciting results. Adapt your shot list as needed, considering factors such as location limitations, actor performances, and time constraints.

In conclusion, developing a shot list is an essential step in the filmmaking process. By meticulously planning your shots, you can effectively communicate your vision, save time and resources, and create a visually compelling film. Remember to collaborate, experiment, and be open to adjustments along the way. Lights, camera, action!

Casting and Auditions

In the exciting world of filmmaking, casting and auditions are crucial components that can make or break a production. In this subchapter, we will delve into the fascinating process of finding the right actors for your film and how to conduct successful auditions. Whether you are a budding filmmaker or a film and media studies student, understanding the intricacies of casting and auditions is essential for creating a successful film.

Firstly, let's explore the importance of casting. The actors chosen for your film play a pivotal role in bringing your vision to life. They are the faces that the audience will connect with and invest their emotions in. Therefore, it is crucial to find actors who not only possess the necessary skills, but also embody the essence of the characters they will portray. Casting involves careful consideration of factors such as physical appearance, acting ability, and chemistry with other cast members. It is the director's responsibility to ensure that the chosen actors align with the overall vision of the film.

Next, we will discuss the process of conducting auditions. Auditions provide an opportunity for actors to showcase their talent and for filmmakers to assess their suitability for specific roles. As a student of film and media studies, understanding how to conduct auditions effectively is vital. This includes creating a welcoming environment, providing clear instructions and expectations, and allowing actors to showcase their unique abilities. Additionally, learning how to provide constructive feedback to actors is essential in helping them grow and improve their craft.

In this subchapter, we will explore various techniques and strategies for casting and auditions. We will discuss the importance of creating a casting call, conducting pre-screenings, and organizing callbacks. We will also touch upon the ethical considerations of casting, such as diversity and representation.

Casting and auditions can be both exhilarating and challenging. However, armed with the knowledge and insights provided in this subchapter, you will be better equipped to navigate this crucial aspect of filmmaking. So, grab your script, prepare your casting call, and get ready to discover the perfect cast for your film. Lights, camera, action - let the casting process begin!

Securing Locations and Permits

When it comes to film production, one of the crucial aspects that can make or break your project is securing the right locations and permits. This subchapter will guide students through the process, ensuring they have a comprehensive understanding of the steps involved in finding suitable filming locations and obtaining the necessary permits.

Finding the perfect location is like finding the missing puzzle piece that completes the picture. It sets the stage for your story, enhances the atmosphere, and adds depth to the overall production value. As a student filmmaker, you may not have access to extravagant sets and backdrops, but don't let that discourage you. There are plenty of unique and affordable locations waiting to be discovered, from public parks and libraries to abandoned buildings and local businesses.

To begin your search, start by brainstorming the specific requirements for each scene in your script. Consider the geographical setting, architectural style, and any unique features necessary for the story's authenticity. Once you have a clear vision, explore your surroundings, keeping an eye out for potential locations that match your criteria. Don't be afraid to get creative – sometimes, unexpected places can turn out to be the perfect backdrop for your film.

Once you've identified potential locations, the next step is obtaining permits. Many countries, states, and even cities have specific regulations and guidelines regarding filming in public spaces. It is essential to research and understand the legal requirements to avoid any legal issues down the line.

Contact the relevant authorities, such as local film commissions or permitting offices, to inquire about the necessary permits and permissions. Be prepared to provide detailed information about your project, including the dates, times, and specific locations you wish to use. It is crucial to start this process well in advance to allow ample time for the paperwork and any required fees.

Additionally, when securing private locations, such as businesses or residences, it is vital to establish clear communication and obtain written agreements. Document any agreements or contracts to protect both parties involved and ensure a smooth filming process.

Remember, securing locations and permits may require patience and persistence. Be prepared for potential rejections or negotiations, but don't give up. As students, you have the advantage of being resourceful and innovative, so embrace the challenge and turn it into an opportunity to showcase your creativity.

In conclusion, securing locations and permits is a critical part of the filmmaking process. By understanding the steps involved and being proactive in your search, you can find the perfect locations that bring your story to life. Remember to always adhere to legal requirements and maintain open communication with location owners. Lights, camera, action – you're one step closer to realizing your directorial vision!

Chapter 3: Production

Setting up the Film Set

When it comes to film production, one of the most crucial aspects is setting up the film set. The film set is the physical space where the scenes of a movie are shot, and it plays a vital role in creating the right atmosphere and bringing the story to life. In this subchapter, we will explore the essential elements and considerations in setting up a film set, providing valuable insights for students interested in film and media studies.

First and foremost, it is important to carefully select the location for your film set. Whether it is an existing structure or a built set, the location should align with the vision of the film and enhance the storytelling. Conducting thorough research and scouting various potential locations will help you find the perfect backdrop for your scenes.

Once the location is finalized, you must focus on the technical aspects of setting up the film set. This includes arranging the lighting, sound equipment, and camera positions to ensure optimal conditions for shooting. It is crucial to work closely with the cinematographer and the sound engineer to determine the best angles and lighting setups for each scene.

Furthermore, attention to detail is key when it comes to production design. The set must be meticulously designed and decorated to reflect the desired time period, mood, and character traits. The production designer plays a vital role in creating a visually captivating and immersive environment that supports the narrative.

Collaboration and effective communication are essential during the process of setting up a film set. The director, production designer, cinematographer, and other members of the crew must work together to bring the director's vision to life. This involves coordinating the placement of props, furniture, and set dressing to ensure consistency and authenticity.

Lastly, safety should never be overlooked on a film set. It is crucial to adhere to safety protocols and ensure the well-being of everyone involved. This includes providing clear instructions for handling equipment, implementing proper lighting precautions, and maintaining a secure working environment.

In conclusion, setting up the film set is a vital component of film production that requires careful planning, attention to detail, and effective collaboration. By selecting the right location, considering technical aspects, focusing on production design, and prioritizing safety, students interested in film and media studies can create captivating and visually appealing film sets that enhance the overall storytelling experience.

Camera Techniques and Movements

In the world of film production and directing, camera techniques and movements play a vital role in conveying the story and capturing the audience's attention. Whether you're a budding filmmaker or a student studying film and media studies, understanding various camera techniques and movements is essential to creating visually captivating and meaningful films.

One of the fundamental camera techniques is framing, which refers to how the subject is positioned within the shot. The choice of framing can greatly impact the audience's perception and emotional response. For example, a close-up shot can emphasize facial expressions, while a wide shot can establish the setting and context. By experimenting with different framing techniques, you can effectively convey the intended message and enhance the storytelling.

Another crucial aspect of camera techniques is camera movement. Camera movements, such as pans, tilts, dollies, and zooms, add dynamism and depth to the visuals. A well-executed camera movement can create a sense of immersion and draw the audience into the narrative. For instance, a tracking shot following a character can generate a feeling of urgency or anticipation. By understanding the purpose and impact of each camera movement, you can enhance the emotional impact and visual aesthetics of your film.

Moreover, camera angles contribute to the overall composition and visual storytelling. Whether it's a high-angle shot to convey vulnerability or a low-angle shot to express dominance, camera angles can add layers of meaning to your film. Experimenting with different camera angles allows you to explore creative perspectives and evoke specific emotions in your audience.

Additionally, mastering the art of camera techniques and movements involves understanding the concept of depth of field. Depth of field refers to the range of distance that appears acceptably sharp within a shot. Adjusting the depth of field can direct the viewer's attention and highlight specific elements within the frame. By manipulating depth of field, you can control the visual hierarchy and guide the audience's gaze.

In conclusion, camera techniques and movements are essential tools for filmmakers and students studying film and media studies. By exploring different framing techniques, camera movements, angles, and depth of field, you can enhance the visual storytelling and captivate your audience. Experimentation, practice, and a keen eye for detail are key to mastering these techniques and creating visually compelling films. So, grab your camera and start exploring the endless possibilities of camera techniques and movements in the world of filmmaking.

Lighting Techniques

In the world of filmmaking, lighting plays a crucial role in setting the mood, creating atmosphere, and enhancing the overall visual appeal of a scene. Whether you are a budding filmmaker or a student of film and media studies, understanding various lighting techniques is essential to elevate your storytelling skills. This subchapter will delve into the different lighting techniques commonly used in film production and directing.

1. Three-Point Lighting: One of the fundamental lighting setups, three-point lighting involves three key components: the key light, fill light, and backlight. The key light is the primary light source, typically placed at a 45-degree angle to the subject. The fill light softens shadows created by the key light, while the backlight adds depth and separation between the subject and the background.

2. High Key Lighting: This technique is characterized by a bright, evenly lit scene with minimal shadows. High key lighting is often used in comedies or upbeat scenes to create a cheerful and light-hearted atmosphere.

3. Low Key Lighting: In contrast to high key lighting, low key lighting creates a moody and dramatic effect by using a minimal amount of light. This technique is commonly employed in film noir or horror genres, where shadows play a significant role in building tension and suspense.

4. Natural Lighting: Harnessing the power of natural light can bring a sense of authenticity and realism to your scenes. Filming during the golden hour (the period shortly after sunrise or before sunset) can

provide a warm and soft glow, perfect for romantic or dreamy sequences.

5. Silhouette Lighting: Silhouette lighting involves positioning the subject in front of a strong light source, such as a window or the sun, resulting in a dark outline against a bright background. This technique is often used to create a sense of mystery or to highlight the shape and form of the subject.

6. Colored Lighting: Adding color to your lighting setup can evoke specific emotions and enhance the visual appeal of a scene. By using gels or colored filters, you can create a unique atmosphere and add depth to your storytelling. For example, blue lighting can convey a sense of tranquility or sadness, while red lighting can evoke tension or danger.

Understanding and mastering these lighting techniques will enable you to effectively convey your story's message and create visually stunning films. Experimentation and practice are key to finding the right lighting setup for each scene, so grab your camera, gather your crew, and let there be light!

Directing Actors

As a film director, one of your primary responsibilities is to bring out the best performances from your actors. Directing actors is both an art and a science, requiring a delicate balance of technical knowledge, emotional intelligence, and effective communication skills. In this subchapter, we will explore the various techniques and strategies you can employ to effectively direct actors and create compelling performances.

Understanding the Craft:

Before diving into the specifics of directing actors, it is essential to have a solid understanding of the craft of acting itself. As a student of film and media studies, you are likely familiar with the basics of acting, but delving deeper into the nuances of the art form will greatly enhance your ability to direct actors. Familiarize yourself with different acting techniques such as Stanislavski's method, Meisner technique, and Strasberg's system, among others. This knowledge will provide you with a common language to communicate with your actors and help you guide their performances.

Building Trust and Collaboration:

Establishing a strong rapport with your actors is crucial for creating a collaborative environment on set. Prioritize building trust and open lines of communication with your performers. Encourage them to share their ideas, interpretations, and concerns about their characters. This collaboration will foster a sense of ownership and investment in their performances, resulting in more authentic and nuanced portrayals.

Effective Communication:

As a director, you must be able to effectively communicate your vision to the actors. Use clear and concise language while providing specific direction. Avoid vague instructions such as "be more emotional" and instead focus on concrete objectives like "convey a sense of sadness in this scene." Utilize visual aids, storyboards, and reference materials to illustrate your ideas visually. Remember that different actors respond to different methods of direction, so be adaptable and find the approach that resonates with each individual.

Creating a Safe and Supportive Environment:

Acting requires vulnerability, and it is your responsibility to create a safe and supportive environment for your actors to explore their characters' emotions. Encourage experimentation and allow for mistakes without judgment. Provide constructive feedback and be open to collaborative solutions. By fostering a positive atmosphere, you will empower your actors to take risks and deliver their best work.

In conclusion, directing actors is a multifaceted task that demands a combination of technical knowledge, emotional intelligence, and effective communication skills. By understanding the craft of acting, building trust and collaboration, employing effective communication techniques, and creating a safe and supportive environment, you can bring out the best performances from your actors. Remember, directing is a constant learning process, so be open to experimentation and always strive for growth.

Sound Recording

In the magical world of filmmaking, sound recording plays a vital role in creating an immersive and captivating experience for the audience. While the visual aspect of a film is undeniably important, sound recording is equally essential in enhancing the overall quality of a film. In this subchapter, we will delve into the intricacies of sound recording, exploring its significance and techniques used in the process.

Sound recording involves capturing and manipulating audio elements that complement the visual aspects of a film. It encompasses the recording of dialogue, ambient sounds, music, and sound effects. The main goal of sound recording is to reproduce and enhance the intended audio experience for the audience, ensuring that every sound is clear, balanced, and synchronized with the visuals.

To achieve high-quality sound recording, filmmakers employ various techniques and tools. One of the primary tools used is the microphone, which captures sound waves and converts them into electrical signals. Different types of microphones are employed for specific purposes, such as lavalier microphones for capturing dialogue, shotgun microphones for focused sound recording, and boom microphones for capturing audio from a distance.

The recording process involves placing microphones strategically to capture sound accurately and minimize background noise. This requires a keen understanding of the environment and the ability to anticipate potential sound-related challenges. Sound recordists often collaborate closely with the director and cinematographer to ensure that the audio is in harmony with the visuals, creating a seamless and immersive experience for the audience.

In addition to capturing dialogue and ambient sounds, sound recording also involves the creation of sound effects and music. Sound effects add depth and realism to a film, while music evokes emotions and sets the tone for various scenes. These elements are carefully integrated into the film during the post-production phase, where sound designers and editors work their magic to create a harmonious blend of audio and visuals.

Understanding the art of sound recording is crucial for aspiring filmmakers and students studying film and media. By mastering this aspect of filmmaking, students can elevate their storytelling abilities and create an immersive cinematic experience for their audience. So, the next time you watch a film, pay close attention to the audio elements, and appreciate the intricate work done behind the scenes to bring them to life.

Chapter 4: Post-production

Importing and Organizing Footage

As aspiring filmmakers, one of the first steps in the film production process is importing and organizing footage. This crucial phase sets the foundation for a well-structured and efficient editing process. In this subchapter, we will delve into the intricacies of importing and organizing footage, providing students in the field of Film and Media Studies with valuable insights and tips.

Importing footage is a fundamental step that requires careful attention to detail. Begin by connecting your camera or storage device to the computer and transferring the files. Ensure you have sufficient storage space and create a designated folder for your project. Organize your footage into separate folders based on scenes or shooting locations. This will streamline the editing process, making it easier to locate specific shots later on.

Once your footage is imported, it is crucial to organize it effectively. Start by creating a clear and consistent naming convention for your files. Include relevant information such as scene number, shot type, and take number. This will eliminate confusion and save time when searching for specific shots during the editing process.

Another key aspect of organizing footage is logging. Logging involves capturing essential information about each shot, such as the timecode, shot description, and any specific details that may be relevant to the scene. This step provides a comprehensive overview of your footage, making it easier to locate specific shots when needed.

In addition to logging, creating a shot list or storyboard can greatly aid in organizing your footage. These visual tools allow you to plan and envision your shots in advance, providing a roadmap for your editing process. A shot list helps ensure that you capture all the necessary shots, while a storyboard provides a visual representation of the desired sequence.

Lastly, consider using software or applications designed specifically for organizing and managing footage. These tools offer features such as tagging, keyword searching, and color coding, making it even easier to locate and sort your footage.

In conclusion, importing and organizing footage is a critical step in the filmmaking process. By following these guidelines, students in the field of Film and Media Studies can ensure a seamless editing process and efficient workflow. Remember, a well-organized project not only saves time but also enhances creativity and allows for a more polished final product. So, take the time to import and organize your footage properly, and let your creativity shine through the lens!

Editing Software and Techniques

In the world of film and media studies, editing plays a crucial role in bringing a story to life. It is the process of selecting, arranging, and modifying various shots and scenes to create a cohesive and engaging narrative. With the advancements in technology, editing software has become an indispensable tool for filmmakers and editors alike. This subchapter will delve into the world of editing software and techniques, providing students with valuable insights and knowledge.

One of the most widely used editing software in the industry is Adobe Premiere Pro. This software offers a plethora of features and tools that enable students to edit their films with precision and creativity. From basic editing functions like cutting and trimming footage to advanced techniques such as color grading and sound mixing, Adobe Premiere Pro provides a comprehensive platform for film editing. Students will learn how to navigate the software, import and organize footage, and apply various effects and transitions to enhance their storytelling.

Another popular editing software is Final Cut Pro, which is exclusive to Apple users. This software offers similar functionalities to Adobe Premiere Pro but with a unique interface and workflow. Students will explore the different tools and techniques offered by Final Cut Pro and understand how to utilize them effectively in their editing process.

In addition to understanding the software, students will also learn various editing techniques that can elevate their films. They will explore the concept of continuity editing, which focuses on maintaining a seamless flow between shots, and learn how to create a rhythm and pacing that enhances the storytelling. Students will also delve into the art of montage editing, which involves juxtaposing shots to convey emotions or ideas. By mastering these techniques, students will have the ability to manipulate time, space, and emotions through their editing choices.

Furthermore, students will be introduced to the concept of non-linear editing, a technique that allows editors to work with multiple shots and scenes simultaneously. They will understand the advantages of non-linear editing over traditional linear editing and learn how to effectively manage their projects using this technique.

Editing software and techniques are essential skills for students studying film and media studies. By mastering these tools and techniques, students will have the ability to shape narratives, evoke emotions, and create compelling stories that captivate audiences.

Adding Visual Effects and Graphics

In today's evolving world of film and media, visual effects and graphics play a crucial role in captivating audiences and bringing stories to life on the big screen. Whether it's a fantastical creature, a breathtaking explosion, or a futuristic cityscape, these elements enhance the overall visual experience and make films more immersive. In this subchapter, we will explore the fascinating world of visual effects and graphics and how they can be seamlessly integrated into your film projects.

Understanding the Basics: Before delving into the intricacies of visual effects and graphics, it is essential to grasp the fundamental concepts. This subchapter will introduce you to the various types of visual effects, such as practical effects, computer-generated imagery (CGI), and motion graphics. You will gain insights into the tools and software commonly used in the industry, including Adobe After Effects, Maya, and Nuke. By understanding these basics, you will be better equipped to plan and execute your visual effects shots.

Creating Engaging Visuals: This subchapter will guide you through the process of creating visually stunning effects and graphics. You will learn about the importance of pre-production planning, including storyboarding and creating visual effects breakdowns. We will discuss techniques for shooting green screen footage and offer tips on lighting and camera setup. Additionally, you will discover how to integrate practical effects with digital elements to achieve seamless results.

Post-Production   Techniques:
Once you have captured your footage, it's time to bring it all together in the post-production stage. This subchapter will walk you through the step-by-step process of compositing, where you will learn how to combine various elements to create a cohesive visual effect. We will also explore color grading and how it can enhance the mood and atmosphere of your film. You will gain insights into sound design and how it can be used to enhance the impact of your visual effects shots.

Case   Studies   and   Industry   Insights:
To provide you with real-world examples and inspiration, this subchapter will include case studies of iconic films known for their exceptional visual effects and graphics. We will explore the groundbreaking work behind movies like "Avatar," "Inception," and "Jurassic Park." Additionally, we will share insights from industry professionals, including visual effects artists and graphic designers, who will provide valuable advice and guidance for aspiring filmmakers.

By the end of this subchapter, you will have a comprehensive understanding of visual effects and graphics and how to incorporate them effectively into your film projects. Armed with this knowledge, you will be able to create visually captivating and engaging films that will leave audiences in awe. So, grab your camera, unleash your creativity, and let the magic of visual effects and graphics take your films to new heights!

Sound Editing and Mixing

In the world of film production, sound plays a crucial role in enhancing the overall cinematic experience. Sound editing and mixing are two essential components that contribute to the final product. This subchapter will delve into the importance of sound editing and mixing, providing students with a comprehensive understanding of these processes.

Sound editing involves the manipulation and organization of sound elements to create a cohesive and immersive audio environment. This process includes the selection and integration of dialogue, music, and sound effects, which are carefully synchronized with the visual elements of the film. Sound editors work closely with the director and other members of the production team to enhance storytelling and evoke specific emotions through sound.

Students pursuing film and media studies must grasp the significance of sound editing in creating a rich and engaging audio experience. Sound effects have the power to transport the audience into different worlds, evoke emotions, and create tension or excitement. By understanding the principles of sound editing, students can effectively utilize sound as a narrative tool.

Once the sound elements are edited, they need to be mixed to achieve a balanced and immersive audio experience. Sound mixing involves adjusting the levels, dynamics, and spatial positioning of various sound elements to create a cohesive and realistic soundscape. Students will learn about the different audio tracks, such as dialogue, music, and effects, and how to manipulate them using specialized software.

Additionally, students will explore the technical aspects of sound editing and mixing, such as equalization, compression, and reverb. These techniques allow for the fine-tuning of audio elements, ensuring that they blend seamlessly and enhance the overall cinematic experience.

To further enhance their understanding, students will also be introduced to the various roles within the sound department, such as sound designers, foley artists, and re-recording mixers. By exploring these roles, students can gain insight into the collaborative nature of sound editing and mixing, as well as the importance of effective communication and teamwork.

In conclusion, sound editing and mixing are integral components of the filmmaking process. By mastering these skills, students can elevate their storytelling abilities and create immersive cinematic experiences. Understanding the principles and techniques of sound editing and mixing is essential for students pursuing film and media studies, as it allows them to effectively utilize sound as a powerful narrative tool.

Color Grading and Finalizing the Film

Color grading and finalizing the film is a crucial step in the post-production process that can greatly enhance the visual storytelling and overall impact of a film. In this subchapter, we will explore the importance of color grading, the techniques involved, and how it contributes to the final product.

Color grading is the process of manipulating and enhancing the colors and tones of a film to create a desired mood or atmosphere. It is an artistic endeavor that requires a keen understanding of color theory, visual aesthetics, and the director's vision for the film. By adjusting the hue, saturation, contrast, and brightness of each shot, color grading can create a cohesive visual style that helps to convey the emotions and themes of the story.

One of the primary goals of color grading is to establish a consistent look throughout the film. This involves matching the colors and tones of different shots to ensure a seamless transition between scenes. For example, a filmmaker may choose to use warm tones and vibrant colors to evoke a sense of nostalgia in a flashback sequence, while opting for cooler tones and desaturated colors to convey a somber mood in a dramatic scene.

There are various tools and software available that facilitate color grading, such as Adobe Premiere Pro, DaVinci Resolve, and Final Cut Pro. These programs offer a range of features, including color wheels, curves, and scopes, which allow filmmakers to fine-tune the color balance and contrast of each shot. Additionally, advanced techniques like color masking and tracking can be employed to selectively adjust specific areas or objects within a frame.

Once the color grading process is complete, the film enters the finalization stage. This involves adding finishing touches such as visual effects, sound design, and audio mixing to enhance the overall cinematic experience. It is important to ensure that the film's color grading aligns with these elements to create a harmonious and immersive final product.

In conclusion, color grading and finalizing the film are vital steps in the post-production process that should not be overlooked. By skillfully manipulating colors and tones, filmmakers can elevate their storytelling and create a visually stunning film. Students studying film and media studies will benefit greatly from understanding the techniques and tools involved in color grading, as it plays a significant role in the overall impact of a film.

Chapter 5: Distribution and Promotion

Film Festivals and Competitions

Film festivals and competitions play a crucial role in the world of filmmaking. They provide a platform for emerging filmmakers to showcase their work, gain recognition, and connect with industry professionals. In this subchapter, we will delve into the significance of film festivals and competitions, their benefits for aspiring filmmakers, and how to navigate these events successfully.

Film festivals are gatherings that celebrate the art of cinema. They bring together industry professionals, film enthusiasts, and students to screen a wide range of films from various genres and countries. These events serve as a hub for networking, knowledge sharing, and industry trends exploration. For students pursuing film and media studies, attending film festivals can be an invaluable experience.

One of the key benefits of film festivals is the exposure they provide to emerging talents. These events often have separate categories for student filmmakers, allowing them to showcase their work and gain recognition. Winning awards at prestigious festivals can open doors to funding opportunities, distribution deals, and crucial industry connections. Moreover, the feedback received from industry professionals and fellow filmmakers can help students grow and improve their craft.

Film festivals also offer a unique opportunity for students to immerse themselves in the world of cinema. By attending screenings, Q&A sessions, and panel discussions, students can gain insights into the creative process, industry trends, and the challenges faced by filmmakers. Additionally, these events often feature workshops and masterclasses conducted by renowned professionals, allowing students to learn from the best in the field.

To make the most of film festivals and competitions, students need to approach them strategically. Researching and selecting the right festivals for their film's genre and theme is crucial. Students should also prepare their marketing materials, such as press kits, posters, and business cards, to leave a lasting impression on industry professionals and potential collaborators.

Attending film festivals can be a costly affair, but students can explore various funding options, such as grants, scholarships, and sponsorships. Additionally, volunteering at festivals can provide students with free access to screenings and networking opportunities.

In conclusion, film festivals and competitions are vital for students pursuing film and media studies. These events offer a platform to showcase their work, gain recognition, and learn from industry professionals. By strategically navigating these events, students can kickstart their careers in the world of filmmaking.

Creating a Film Marketing Plan

In today's competitive film industry, a well-executed marketing plan is essential for the success of any film. Whether you're an aspiring filmmaker or studying film and media, understanding how to create an effective film marketing plan is crucial. This subchapter will guide you through the process of developing a comprehensive marketing strategy to promote your film and reach your target audience.

1. Identifying your target audience: Before diving into marketing tactics, it's important to identify who your film is intended for. Consider the genre, themes, and demographic that your film appeals to. This will help you tailor your marketing efforts and reach the right audience.

2. Defining your film's unique selling proposition (USP): What makes your film stand out from the rest? Identify the key elements that differentiate your film from others in the market. Whether it's a compelling story, unique visuals, or talented actors, understanding your film's USP will help you communicate its value to your target audience.

3. Developing a marketing budget: Determine the financial resources available for marketing your film. Allocating a budget will help you prioritize marketing activities, such as social media campaigns, public relations, advertising, and film festivals.

4. Crafting a compelling marketing message: Create a captivating tagline or elevator pitch that summarizes your film's essence in a concise and engaging manner. This message will be the foundation of

your marketing materials and should resonate with your target audience.

5. Utilizing social media and online platforms: Leverage the power of social media to build buzz around your film. Create dedicated profiles on platforms like Facebook, Twitter, Instagram, and YouTube to share behind-the-scenes content, trailers, and exclusive updates. Engage with your audience, respond to comments, and encourage them to share your film with their networks.

6. Leveraging traditional marketing channels: While online platforms are essential, don't overlook traditional marketing channels. Consider print advertisements, radio interviews, press releases, and collaborations with local businesses or organizations to expand your film's reach.

7. Partnering with influencers and film festivals: Collaborate with influencers, bloggers, and YouTubers who have a following in the film and media niche. Their endorsement can help generate buzz and attract attention to your film. Additionally, submit your film to relevant film festivals to gain exposure and potentially secure distribution deals.

Remember, a film marketing plan is not a one-size-fits-all approach, and it should be tailored to your specific film and target audience. By understanding your audience, defining your film's USP, and utilizing both online and traditional marketing channels, you can effectively promote your film and increase its chances of success in the competitive film industry.

Utilizing Social Media and Online Platforms

In today's digital age, social media and online platforms have become invaluable tools for filmmakers and aspiring directors. The power of social media lies in its ability to connect with audiences, promote your work, and build a strong online presence. This subchapter will guide students in the film and media studies niche on how to effectively harness the potential of social media and online platforms to enhance their careers in film production and directing.

1. Building a Personal Brand: Creating a strong personal brand is crucial in the film industry. Students can learn how to craft a compelling online persona that reflects their unique style and vision as filmmakers. This subchapter will provide practical tips and strategies on developing a consistent brand across various social media platforms, such as Instagram, Twitter, and YouTube.

2. Engaging with Audiences: Social media platforms offer a direct line of communication with audiences. Students will discover ways to engage with their target audience, build a loyal fan base, and receive feedback on their work. Techniques like hosting live Q&A sessions, sharing behind-the-scenes content, and running contests will be explored to foster a sense of community and increase audience engagement.

3. Promoting Film Projects: Whether it's a short film, a documentary, or a feature-length movie, social media can serve as a powerful promotional tool. This subchapter will delve into effective strategies for marketing and promoting film

projects on social media platforms. Students will learn how to create compelling content, leverage hashtags, collaborate with influencers, and utilize paid advertising to reach a wider audience.

4. Networking and Collaboration: Social media opens doors to networking opportunities with industry professionals and potential collaborators. This subchapter will guide students on how to establish meaningful connections through platforms like LinkedIn and film-specific online communities. Tips on approaching industry experts, seeking mentorship, and finding potential crew members will be shared.

5. Online Learning and Resources: The internet offers a wealth of resources for aspiring filmmakers. This subchapter will introduce students to online platforms that provide film-related courses, tutorials, and forums for knowledge sharing. Students will gain insights into the best platforms for expanding their skill set, learning about industry trends, and staying up to date with the latest technological advancements.

In conclusion, harnessing the power of social media and online platforms is essential for students in the film and media studies niche. By building a personal brand, engaging with audiences, promoting film projects, networking, and utilizing online learning resources, students can pave the way for a successful career in film production and directing.

Film Distribution Options

Once a film is completed, the next crucial step in the filmmaking process is distribution. Film distribution refers to the process of making a film available for viewing by an audience. It involves getting the film into cinemas, on television, streaming platforms, or even DVD and Blu-ray. In this subchapter, we will explore the various film distribution options available to filmmakers.

1. Theatrical Release: One of the most traditional and widely recognized distribution methods is a theatrical release. This involves screening the film in cinemas, allowing audiences to experience it on the big screen. Theatrical releases are ideal for big-budget films with a wide appeal and can generate significant revenue.

2. Television: Television distribution involves selling the rights of the film to television networks or cable channels. This option allows for a wider audience reach, as television is a common medium for viewership. Filmmakers may opt for a TV release if their film caters to a specific genre or target audience.

3. Streaming Platforms: With the rise of digital technology, streaming platforms have become increasingly popular for film distribution. Platforms like Netflix, Amazon Prime Video, and Hulu provide filmmakers with a global audience and the potential for long-term revenues. Streaming platforms are particularly advantageous for independent filmmakers, as they offer greater exposure and accessibility.

4. DVD and Blu-ray: Although physical media is not as popular as it once was, DVD and Blu-ray distribution still have a place in the film

industry. Filmmakers can produce DVDs or Blu-ray discs and sell them directly to consumers or through retail outlets. This option is suitable for niche or specialized films that may not find a wide audience through other distribution channels.

5. Online Platforms: In addition to streaming services, filmmakers can distribute their films online through platforms like Vimeo, YouTube, or their own websites. This option allows for greater control over the distribution process and can be an effective way to reach a specific target audience or build a fanbase.

It is important for students studying film and media studies to understand these distribution options as they are essential for getting their work seen by a wider audience. Each distribution method has its own pros and cons, and filmmakers should carefully consider their goals, target audience, and budget when deciding on the most suitable distribution strategy for their film.

Building a Portfolio and Resume

In the competitive world of film and media studies, having a strong portfolio and resume is essential for aspiring filmmakers and directors. Your portfolio showcases your skills, creativity, and experience, while your resume highlights your education, training, and professional background. This subchapter will guide students through the process of building an impressive portfolio and resume that will grab the attention of potential employers and collaborators.

1.   Crafting   a   Portfolio: Your portfolio is a visual representation of your work and should reflect your unique style and creativity. Include a variety of projects that highlight your skills in different areas of film production and directing. This may include short films, music videos, commercials, or even photography. Be selective and choose your best work to showcase.

2.   Organizing   Your   Portfolio: Ensure that your portfolio is well-organized and easy to navigate. Divide your work into categories such as directing, cinematography, editing, and screenwriting. Consider creating an online portfolio website or using platforms like Vimeo or YouTube to showcase your videos. Include a brief description of each project, highlighting your role and responsibilities.

3.   Showcasing   Technical   Skills: Demonstrate your technical skills by including projects that showcase your proficiency in camera operation, lighting, sound design, and

post-production. If you have specialized skills such as animation or visual effects, include samples of your work in these areas as well.

4.	Collaboration	and	Teamwork: Film production is a collaborative process, so it's important to demonstrate your ability to work well with others. Include projects where you collaborated with a team, highlighting your role as a director or production crew member. Mention any awards or recognition received for your work.

5.	Building	a	Resume: Your resume should complement your portfolio by providing a concise overview of your education, training, and professional experience. Include your contact information, education details, relevant coursework, and any film-related workshops or certifications you have completed.

6.	Highlighting	Experience: Include any internships, part-time jobs, or volunteer work in the film industry. Even if your experience is limited, highlight transferable skills such as leadership, problem-solving, and attention to detail.

7.	References	and	Recommendations: Include references or recommendations from professors, mentors, or industry professionals who can vouch for your skills and work ethic. These endorsements can add credibility to your resume.

Remember, building a portfolio and resume is an ongoing process. Continuously update and refine your portfolio as you gain more experience and complete new projects. Stay up-to-date with industry trends and technologies to demonstrate your commitment to growth and improvement.

By following these guidelines, students pursuing film and media studies will be well-equipped to showcase their talents and stand out in a competitive industry.

Chapter 6: Case Studies

Analyzing Successful Film Productions

In the ever-evolving world of film and media, it is crucial for students studying film and media studies to analyze successful film productions. By delving deep into the intricacies of these films, students can gain valuable insights into the art and craft of filmmaking. This subchapter aims to provide students with a comprehensive guide on how to analyze successful film productions and extract valuable lessons from them.

The first step in analyzing successful film productions is to carefully watch and observe the film. As students, it is important to pay attention to various elements such as the narrative structure, cinematography, mise-en-scène, editing, sound design, and acting performances. By focusing on these aspects, students can begin to understand how each element contributes to the overall impact and success of the film.

Furthermore, students should explore the historical and cultural context in which the film was produced. Understanding the social and political climate during the making of the film can shed light on the motivations and intentions of the filmmakers. It is also beneficial to research the director, writer, and key crew members to gain a deeper understanding of their artistic vision and filmmaking style.

In addition to the technical and contextual analysis, students should also analyze the film's themes, symbolism, and underlying messages. By critically examining these aspects, students can uncover the deeper layers of meaning and engage in thoughtful discussions about the film's social, cultural, or philosophical implications.

Furthermore, students should not limit their analysis to only successful mainstream films but also explore independent, international, and avant-garde cinema. By broadening their exposure to different types of films, students can develop a more comprehensive understanding of the diverse approaches and techniques employed by filmmakers worldwide.

Finally, it is crucial for students to engage in discussions and debates with their peers and instructors. By sharing their interpretations and insights, students can gain different perspectives and deepen their understanding of the film. These discussions can also help students refine their analytical skills and develop a critical eye for filmmaking.

In conclusion, analyzing successful film productions is an essential aspect of studying film and media studies. By closely examining various elements of a film, exploring its historical and cultural context, and engaging in discussions, students can acquire a comprehensive understanding of the art and craft of filmmaking. This subchapter provides students with the necessary tools and methodologies to conduct meaningful analyses of successful film productions, ultimately enriching their knowledge and appreciation of the cinematic medium.

Examining the Directing Styles of Renowned Directors

In the captivating world of film production and directing, there are certain individuals who have left an indelible mark on the industry with their unique and groundbreaking directing styles. These directors have not only created timeless masterpieces but have also shaped the way we perceive and understand cinema. In this subchapter, we delve into the directing styles of renowned directors, exploring their distinctive approaches and techniques that have made them icons in the field.

One director whose style has had a profound impact on the film industry is Alfred Hitchcock. Known as the "Master of Suspense," Hitchcock's meticulous attention to detail and his ability to create tension and suspense are unparalleled. His use of innovative camera angles, such as the famous "Hitchcock zoom," and his mastery of suspenseful storytelling have inspired countless filmmakers to this day.

Another director who has left an indelible mark on cinema is Quentin Tarantino. Tarantino's directing style is characterized by his nonlinear storytelling, eclectic mix of genres, and his signature use of violence. His films often feature rich dialogue, memorable characters, and intricate plotlines that keep audiences engaged from start to finish. Tarantino's unique ability to blend pop culture references with his own distinctive vision has made him a true auteur.

Steven Spielberg, one of the most successful directors in history, is renowned for his ability to tell emotionally resonant stories. Spielberg's directing style often focuses on themes of childhood, adventure, and the power of imagination. His visual storytelling, use of music, and expert pacing have made him a master storyteller, capable of creating films that touch the hearts of audiences around the world.

Examining the directing styles of these renowned directors not only provides insight into their creative processes but also offers valuable lessons for aspiring filmmakers. By studying their techniques, students can gain a deeper understanding of the art of directing, and how to effectively communicate their vision to the audience.

In conclusion, the directing styles of renowned directors like Alfred Hitchcock, Quentin Tarantino, and Steven Spielberg offer a wealth of knowledge and inspiration for students studying film and media studies. Their unique approaches and techniques have not only influenced the industry but have also elevated the art of filmmaking to new heights. By exploring their directing styles, students can gain valuable insights into the creative process and learn how to effectively convey their own visions on the screen. Lights, Camera, Action indeed!

Learning from Film Production Mistakes

When it comes to film production, mistakes are bound to happen. Whether you are a seasoned filmmaker or just starting out, it is important to remember that mistakes are not failures but valuable learning opportunities. In this subchapter, we will explore some common film production mistakes and how you can learn from them to improve your craft.

One of the most common mistakes in film production is poor planning. Many students often underestimate the importance of pre-production, rushing into shooting without a solid plan. This can lead to wasted time, resources, and ultimately, a subpar end product. By taking the time to thoroughly plan your film, you can avoid costly mistakes and ensure smoother production.

Another mistake often made by students is neglecting the importance of communication and collaboration. Film production is a team effort, requiring effective communication between all members involved. Lack of communication can result in misunderstandings, delays, and overall chaos on set. By fostering a collaborative environment and maintaining open lines of communication, you can avoid unnecessary mistakes and create a more cohesive film.

Technical errors are also common in film production, especially for students who may not have access to high-end equipment or professional training. However, instead of being discouraged by these limitations, students should embrace them as opportunities for creativity. Learning how to work with limited resources and adapt to technical challenges will not only enhance your problem-solving skills but also push your creativity to new heights.

Lastly, one of the biggest mistakes in film production is neglecting the importance of post-production. Many students focus solely on capturing footage but overlook the crucial role of editing and sound design in creating a compelling film. By dedicating ample time and effort to post-production, you can refine your film and bring out its full potential.

In conclusion, mistakes are an inevitable part of film production, but they should not be seen as failures. Instead, they offer valuable lessons that can propel your growth as a filmmaker. By recognizing common mistakes such as poor planning, lack of communication, technical errors, and neglecting post-production, students in the field of film and media studies can learn from these experiences and improve their craft. So, embrace mistakes, learn from them, and let them guide you towards becoming a better filmmaker.

Collaborating with a Film Crew

In the exciting world of film production, collaboration is key. No film can be made without a dedicated and skilled crew working together as a well-oiled machine. Whether you aspire to be a director, cinematographer, or any other role in the industry, understanding how to effectively collaborate with a film crew is essential. This subchapter will provide valuable insights and tips on how to foster a positive working relationship with your fellow crew members.

First and foremost, communication is the backbone of any successful collaboration. As a student filmmaker, it is crucial to establish clear lines of communication with your crew members from the very beginning. Regular meetings and discussions will ensure that everyone is on the same page and working towards the same vision. Encourage an open and respectful environment where ideas and concerns can be shared freely.

Another important aspect of collaborating with a film crew is understanding and respecting each individual's role and expertise. Every member of the crew brings a unique skill set to the table, and acknowledging and appreciating their contributions will foster a sense of unity and motivation. Remember, filmmaking is a team effort, and each crew member's role is vital in achieving the desired end result.

Additionally, effective collaboration involves being adaptable and flexible. Circumstances on set can change unexpectedly, and being able to adjust and problem-solve on the spot is crucial. Encourage your crew members to brainstorm and think creatively when faced with challenges. Embracing spontaneity and being open to new ideas can lead to unexpected and innovative solutions.

Lastly, it is essential to create a positive and supportive work environment. Film production can be stressful and demanding, but fostering a sense of camaraderie and appreciation for each other's efforts will go a long way in maintaining morale. Recognize and celebrate the achievements of your crew members, no matter how small. A united and motivated crew will not only produce better work but will also create an enjoyable and fulfilling filmmaking experience for everyone involved.

In conclusion, collaborating with a film crew is an integral part of the filmmaking process. By establishing effective communication, respecting each other's roles, adapting to unexpected situations, and creating a positive work environment, you will set yourself up for success in the exciting world of film production. Remember, teamwork makes the dream work!

Showcasing Student Film Projects

As a student pursuing a degree in Film and Media Studies, one of the most exciting aspects of your academic journey will be the opportunity to showcase your own film projects. This subchapter serves as a guide to help you navigate the process of presenting your work to an audience and maximizing its impact.

1.   Film   Festivals   and   Competitions: Film festivals and competitions provide an excellent platform to showcase your student film projects. Research local, national, and international events that accept student submissions. Submit your work to these festivals and competitions to gain valuable exposure and recognition. Winning or even participating in such events can open doors to future opportunities and networking within the industry.

2.   Campus   Screenings: Many universities and colleges have dedicated spaces for screening student films. These events not only allow you to share your work with peers and faculty but also provide valuable feedback and constructive criticism. Collaborate with your department or film club to organize regular screenings, inviting fellow students, professors, and even industry professionals to attend. This will help you build a reputation as a filmmaker and gain valuable insights from the audience's reactions.

3.   Online   Platforms: In today's digital age, online platforms offer a vast audience reach for showcasing student film projects. Create a YouTube or Vimeo channel to upload and share your work. Utilize social media platforms such as

Instagram, Twitter, and Facebook to promote your films and engage with potential viewers. Collaborate with other student filmmakers to cross-promote each other's work and build a supportive online community.

4. Film Showcases and Exhibitions: Consider organizing your own film showcase or exhibition on campus or in your local community. This allows you to curate a program of student films, creating a cohesive experience for viewers. Invite friends, family, professors, and industry professionals to attend these events, providing an opportunity for networking and feedback.

5. Alumni Networks and Connections: Tap into the alumni network of your film department or program. Reach out to graduates who have successfully transitioned into the film industry and seek their guidance. They can offer advice on how to effectively showcase your work and may even help you connect with industry professionals or secure internships.

Remember, showcasing your student film projects is not only about gaining recognition but also about learning and growing as a filmmaker. Embrace feedback, celebrate your achievements, and continue to refine your craft. With passion, perseverance, and a strategic approach, your student film projects can pave the way for a successful future in the film and media industry.

Chapter 7: Resources and Further Learning

Recommended Books and Websites

As a student studying film and media studies, it is crucial to have access to the right resources that can enhance your knowledge and understanding of the subject. Whether you are interested in film production, directing, or simply want to broaden your understanding of the industry, here are some recommended books and websites that will be invaluable to your journey.

Books:

1. "The Filmmaker's Handbook: A Comprehensive Guide for the Digital Age" by Steven Ascher and Edward Pincus - This book is an essential tool for anyone interested in filmmaking. It covers all aspects of the production process, from pre-production to post-production, and provides valuable insights into the technical and artistic aspects of filmmaking.

2. "In the Blink of an Eye: A Perspective on Film Editing" by Walter Murch - This book delves into the art of film editing and offers a unique perspective on the role of the editor in shaping the narrative. Murch, an Academy Award-winning editor, shares his experiences and provides valuable insights into the creative process.

3. "Directing: Film Techniques and Aesthetics" by Michael Rabiger - This book is a comprehensive guide to the art and craft of directing. It explores various directing techniques, covers the fundamentals of storytelling, and provides practical advice for aspiring directors.

Websites:

1. The American Film Institute (AFI) - AFI's website offers a wealth of resources for film students, including interviews, articles, and educational materials. It also provides information about scholarships and grants for aspiring filmmakers.

2. Film School Rejects - This website offers a fresh and insightful perspective on the world of film and media. It features reviews, interviews, and articles on a wide range of topics, from film analysis to industry trends.

3. No Film School - No Film School is a popular website that offers tutorials, interviews, and industry news. It covers various aspects of filmmaking, including cinematography, screenwriting, and post-production.

By exploring these recommended books and websites, you will gain a deeper understanding of film production and directing. They will provide you with valuable insights, practical advice, and inspiration from industry professionals. Remember, the key to success in film and media studies is continuous learning and staying updated with the latest trends and techniques. Happy reading and exploring!

Film Production and Directing Courses

Lights, Camera, Action: A Student's Handbook to Film Production and Directing

Lights, Camera, Action: A Student's Handbook to Film Production and Directing is a comprehensive guide designed specifically for students pursuing a career in film and media studies. This subchapter focuses on the various courses available in film production and directing, providing valuable insights into the journey of becoming a successful filmmaker.

Film production and directing courses are essential for anyone aspiring to enter the dynamic and ever-evolving world of filmmaking. These courses provide students with a solid foundation in all aspects of filmmaking, from pre-production to post-production.

The curriculum of film production courses typically covers a wide range of topics, including scriptwriting, cinematography, production design, sound design, editing, and film theory. Students will learn about the technical and creative aspects of filmmaking, gaining hands-on experience in using professional-grade equipment and software.

Directing courses focus on developing the skills necessary to bring a vision to life on the screen. Students will learn about shot composition, visual storytelling, working with actors, and managing a film set. Additionally, courses may delve into the intricacies of film genres, directing styles, and the history of cinema to provide students with a well-rounded education.

One of the key advantages of these courses is the opportunity to collaborate with fellow students on film projects. This fosters a creative and collaborative environment, allowing aspiring filmmakers to build a strong network and gain valuable experience working as part of a team.

Film production and directing courses also often include practical elements such as internships and industry placements. These opportunities allow students to apply their knowledge in real-world settings, working alongside industry professionals and gaining invaluable insights into the industry.

Upon completion of film production and directing courses, students will be equipped with the skills and knowledge necessary to pursue a career in the film and media industry. They will have a solid understanding of the filmmaking process, from concept development to distribution, and will be prepared to take on various roles in the industry, such as directors, producers, cinematographers, or editors.

In conclusion, film production and directing courses play a crucial role in shaping aspiring filmmakers into successful professionals. Lights, Camera, Action: A Student's Handbook to Film Production and Directing provides a comprehensive overview of the courses available, offering valuable guidance to students pursuing a career in film and media studies.

Joining Film Clubs and Organizations

Film clubs and organizations are a valuable resource for students interested in film and media studies. These groups provide a platform for like-minded individuals to come together, share ideas, and collaborate on projects. By joining a film club or organization, students can gain practical experience, expand their network, and enhance their understanding of the film industry. In this subchapter, we will explore the benefits of joining film clubs and organizations and provide guidance on how to find and get involved with these groups.

One of the main advantages of joining a film club or organization is the opportunity to gain hands-on experience. Many clubs organize workshops, film screenings, and production projects, allowing students to put their theoretical knowledge into practice. By actively participating in these activities, students can develop their filmmaking skills, learn new techniques, and refine their creative vision. Furthermore, collaborating with fellow club members fosters teamwork and provides a supportive environment for growth.

Another benefit of joining film clubs and organizations is the chance to build a network within the film industry. These groups often host events that bring together industry professionals, allowing students to establish connections and learn from experienced individuals. Networking opportunities can lead to internships, job opportunities, and mentorship, providing valuable insights into the industry and potential career paths. Additionally, being part of a film club or organization can enhance a student's resume, demonstrating their passion and commitment to their field of study.

Finding film clubs and organizations is easier than ever, thanks to the internet and social media platforms. Students can start by researching local film clubs at their school or in their community. Many universities have film societies or clubs dedicated to film and media studies. Additionally, online platforms like Meetup and Facebook groups can help students find like-minded individuals in their area. Attending film festivals, industry conferences, and seminars is another way to connect with individuals and discover new organizations to join.

In conclusion, joining film clubs and organizations is a valuable step for students pursuing film and media studies. By participating in these groups, students can gain practical experience, expand their network, and enhance their understanding of the film industry. Whether it's through workshops, screenings, or collaborative projects, film clubs offer a supportive environment for growth and creativity. So, don't hesitate to join a film club or organization and take your passion for film to the next level.

Networking Opportunities

In the world of film and media studies, networking is an essential skill that can open doors and create endless possibilities for your future career. Whether you aspire to be a film producer, director, or any other role in the industry, building a strong network can greatly enhance your chances of success. This subchapter explores the various networking opportunities available to students in the field of film and media studies.

1. Film Festivals: Attending film festivals is a fantastic way to connect with industry professionals, fellow students, and film enthusiasts. These events provide a platform for showcasing your work, discussing films with like-minded individuals, and establishing valuable connections. Take advantage of the networking sessions, panel discussions, and workshops that are often part of film festivals, as they offer opportunities to meet potential mentors and collaborators.

2. Industry Conferences: Many film and media conferences are organized annually, bringing together professionals from various sectors of the industry. Participating in these conferences can expose you to the latest trends, technologies, and industry insights while allowing you to meet influential figures. Make sure to attend sessions and engage in conversations with experts during breaks and networking events.

3. Student Film Organizations: Joining a student film organization or club can provide you with a supportive community and networking opportunities. These groups often organize film screenings, workshops, and guest lectures, allowing you to meet fellow students

and industry professionals. Engage actively in these organizations, as they can serve as a stepping stone towards internships and other career-building opportunities.

4. Internships and Workshops: Seek out internships and workshops offered by production companies, film studios, and media organizations. These experiences not only provide valuable hands-on learning but also allow you to meet professionals already working in the industry. Building relationships with your supervisors and colleagues during internships can lead to future job opportunities or recommendations.

5. Online Platforms: In this digital age, online platforms such as LinkedIn, film-specific forums, and social media groups can be powerful networking tools. Create a professional online presence, share your work, and engage in conversations with industry professionals. These platforms offer a convenient way to connect with individuals from all over the world, expanding your network beyond geographical limitations.

Remember, networking is not just about making connections but also about maintaining them. Follow up with the people you meet, express your gratitude, and stay in touch. Networking is a continuous process, and nurturing relationships can lead to long-term partnerships, mentorships, and collaborative opportunities. Embrace networking opportunities with enthusiasm, as they can be the key to unlocking a successful career in film and media studies.

Internships and Job Opportunities in the Film Industry

In today's highly competitive job market, internships have become an essential stepping stone for students pursuing a career in the film industry. These opportunities not only provide hands-on experience but also allow students to network with industry professionals, gain valuable industry insights, and build a strong foundation for their future careers. This subchapter explores the various internships and job opportunities available in the film industry, providing students with a comprehensive guide to jumpstart their professional journey.

1. Understanding Internships: This section introduces students to the concept of internships and their significance in the film industry. It emphasizes the importance of internships as a means to gain practical experience, develop skills, and make industry connections.

2. Types of Internships: Here, students will discover the different types of internships available in the film industry, such as production internships, post-production internships, and film festival internships. Each type is explained in detail, highlighting the specific responsibilities and skills required for each role.

3. Finding Internships: This section provides practical advice on how to find the best internships in the film industry. It explores various resources, such as online job boards, industry-specific websites, and networking events, offering students useful tips on crafting a compelling resume and cover letter.

4. Job Opportunities: Beyond internships, this section delves into the wide range of job opportunities available in the film industry. From production assistants and camera operators to film editors and

directors, students will gain a comprehensive understanding of the various roles they can pursue.

5. Industry Insights: To help students navigate the film industry successfully, this section offers valuable insights from industry professionals. These insights touch upon crucial topics like the current state of the industry, emerging trends, and the skills and qualities that employers seek in candidates.

6. Building a Successful Career: In the final section, students will learn how to leverage their internships and job opportunities to build a successful career in the film industry. It provides guidance on networking, professional development, and continuous learning, emphasizing the importance of perseverance and passion.

By the end of this subchapter, students will have a solid understanding of internships and job opportunities in the film industry. They will be equipped with the knowledge and resources to pursue their dreams and embark on a successful career in film and media. This subchapter is a valuable guide for students in film and media studies, helping them navigate the industry and make informed decisions about their future.

Chapter 8: Conclusion

Reflecting on the Journey of Film Production and Directing

As students of film and media studies, we embark on a remarkable journey into the fascinating world of film production and directing. In this subchapter, we take a moment to reflect on this incredible journey, exploring the challenges, triumphs, and lessons learned along the way.

The path of film production and directing is an exciting and dynamic one, filled with numerous possibilities and opportunities for growth. It is a creative process that requires dedication, passion, and a deep understanding of the craft. Whether you have dreams of becoming the next Scorsese or Spielberg or simply want to explore your artistic side, this journey will undoubtedly shape you as a filmmaker and storyteller.

One of the first lessons we encounter on this journey is the importance of collaboration. Film production is a team effort, and the director acts as the captain, guiding the ship towards its destination. We learn to work closely with cinematographers, editors, sound engineers, and actors, among others, to bring our visions to life. This collaborative process teaches us the value of effective communication, compromise, and trust, as we learn to navigate the challenges that arise during production.

Additionally, we discover the significance of pre-production planning. From script development to storyboarding, location scouting to casting, every step in the pre-production phase contributes to the success of the final product. Through careful planning and attention to detail, we lay the groundwork for a smooth and efficient shoot, ensuring that our vision is effectively translated onto the screen.

During the production phase, we encounter the exhilaration and chaos of bringing our ideas to life. From managing tight schedules and budgets to troubleshooting unexpected challenges, we learn to think on our feet and adapt to the ever-changing demands of the set. These experiences teach us resilience, problem-solving skills, and the ability to make quick decisions under pressure – all essential qualities for a successful director.

Finally, as we near the end of our journey, we delve into the world of post-production. Here, we uncover the magic of editing, sound design, and visual effects, discovering how these elements can enhance our storytelling and evoke emotion in our audience. We learn the importance of patience and attention to detail, as we meticulously fine-tune every frame to create a polished and impactful final product.

In conclusion, the journey of film production and directing is a transformative one, shaping us not only as filmmakers but also as individuals. It is a journey of self-discovery, creativity, and growth, where we learn to harness our imagination and bring our stories to life. As students of film and media studies, we are fortunate to embark on this extraordinary adventure, and by reflecting on our experiences, we can truly appreciate the artistry and craftsmanship behind every film we watch.

Continuing to Grow as a Filmmaker

As a student in film and media studies, your journey as a filmmaker is just beginning. It's important to recognize that learning in this field is a continuous process that extends far beyond the classroom. In this subchapter, we will explore the various ways you can continue to grow as a filmmaker and hone your skills in pursuit of your dreams.

1. Embrace Lifelong Learning: The world of film is constantly evolving, so it's crucial to stay updated on the latest techniques, technologies, and trends. Attend film festivals, workshops, and seminars, and read books and articles written by industry professionals. By immersing yourself in the ever-evolving landscape of cinema, you'll expand your knowledge and open yourself up to new ideas.

2. Collaborate with Peers: Filmmaking is a collaborative art form, and working with fellow students can be a valuable learning experience. Forming a creative group or joining a film club will allow you to share ideas, exchange feedback, and collaborate on projects. The diversity of perspectives will enhance your understanding of storytelling and help you develop your own unique voice.

3. Seek Mentorship: Finding a mentor who shares your passion for filmmaking can provide invaluable guidance and support. Look for experienced filmmakers, professors, or industry professionals who can offer insights into the craft and provide constructive criticism. Their mentorship can help you navigate the challenges of the industry and provide you with a sense of direction.

4. Create Your Own Opportunities: Don't wait for opportunities to come to you; create them yourself. Start by making short films, documentaries, or even experimental projects. Use social media platforms to share your work and seek feedback from a wider audience. The more you create, the more you will refine your skills and build a portfolio that showcases your talent.

5. Learn from Failure: Filmmaking is a process filled with ups and downs. It's essential to embrace failure as a learning opportunity rather than a setback. Analyze your mistakes, seek constructive criticism, and use them as stepping stones toward improvement. Remember that even the most successful filmmakers have faced setbacks, but it is their resilience and determination that have led them to success.

In conclusion, continuing to grow as a filmmaker is a lifelong journey that requires dedication, passion, and an open mind. By embracing lifelong learning, collaborating with peers, seeking mentorship, creating your own opportunities, and learning from failure, you will constantly evolve as a filmmaker. Embrace the challenges, embrace the learning, and most importantly, embrace the incredible journey that awaits you in the world of filmmaking.

Inspiring Others through Film

In the world of film and media studies, one of the most powerful aspects of the craft is its ability to inspire and influence others. Through the magic of storytelling and the visual medium, filmmakers have the unique opportunity to touch the hearts and minds of their audience, creating a lasting impact that can shape perspectives and ignite change.

The art of inspiring others through film goes beyond mere entertainment. It is about connecting with people on a deeper level, provoking emotions, and challenging societal norms. As students of film production and directing, you have the incredible opportunity to harness the power of this art form to make a difference in the world.

One of the key ways to inspire others through film is by telling stories that resonate with universal themes. Whether it's a tale of overcoming adversity, celebrating the triumph of the human spirit, or shedding light on social issues, stories that connect with the audience's emotions have the potential to leave a lasting impression. By understanding the power of storytelling, you can craft narratives that touch the hearts of viewers, leaving them inspired and motivated.

Another way to inspire others is through the visual language of film. As filmmakers, you have the ability to create stunning visuals that can captivate and transport viewers to different worlds. Whether it's through the use of color, composition, or visual effects, the visual aspect of filmmaking can evoke powerful emotions and inspire awe in your audience. By mastering the art of visual storytelling, you can create a cinematic experience that not only entertains but also inspires and leaves a lasting impact.

Furthermore, the role of filmmakers as influencers cannot be underestimated. By addressing important social issues through your films, you can raise awareness and inspire action. Whether it's shedding light on environmental concerns, advocating for social justice, or promoting inclusivity, your films have the power to spark conversations and drive positive change. By using your platform responsibly and thoughtfully, you can inspire others to take action and make a difference in the world.

In conclusion, the subchapter "Inspiring Others through Film" highlights the immense power of the art form to touch hearts, challenge perspectives, and influence change. As students of film and media studies, you have the opportunity to harness this power and create films that inspire, provoke, and leave a lasting impact on your audience. By mastering the art of storytelling, visual language, and using your platform responsibly, you can truly make a difference in the world through your films.

Final Thoughts and Words of Encouragement

As we come to the end of this handbook, it is important to reflect on the incredible journey you have embarked upon as students of film and media studies. Throughout this book, we have explored the vast world of film production and directing, delving into the technical aspects, creative processes, and the immense dedication it takes to bring a story to life on the silver screen. Now, it is time to offer some final thoughts and words of encouragement to inspire you on your own filmmaking quest.

First and foremost, always remember the power of storytelling. Film has the ability to captivate, educate, and inspire audiences like no other medium. As students of this craft, you have a unique opportunity to share your voice and vision with the world. Embrace this power and use it to tell stories that matter, stories that have the potential to make a difference in people's lives.

Never underestimate the importance of collaboration. Filmmaking is a team effort, and the relationships you build with your crew members, actors, and fellow students are crucial to your success. Embrace the diversity of ideas and perspectives that come with working with others, and always be open to learning from those around you. Remember, the best ideas often emerge from the collective wisdom of a group.

Perseverance is key in this industry. Filmmaking is not for the faint of heart; it requires resilience, determination, and the ability to weather the inevitable storms that come with the creative process. There will be setbacks, challenges, and moments of self-doubt, but it is in these moments that true growth occurs. Embrace failure as a stepping stone towards success and never lose sight of your passion for the craft.

Lastly, always be a student. The world of film and media is ever-evolving, and it is essential to stay curious, adaptable, and hungry for knowledge. Seek out new techniques, study the work of masters, and continue to refine your skills. The more you learn, the more you will grow as a filmmaker.

In conclusion, as you embark on your journey into the world of film production and directing, remember to cherish the magic of storytelling, embrace collaboration, persevere through challenges, and never stop learning. You have chosen a path that requires immense dedication, but with passion and hard work, the possibilities are endless. Lights, camera, action - go forth and create your own cinematic masterpieces!